道德經

Lao Zi
Dao De Jing

Translated with a thematic reading guide by Wang Keping

FOREIGN LANGUAGES PRESS

First Edition 2008

Translated with a thematic reading guide by
Wang Keping

ISBN 978-7-119-03445-4
©Foreign Languages Press, Beijing, China, 2008

Published by Foreign Languages Press
24 Baiwanzhuang Road, Beijing 100037, China
Website: http://www.flp.com.cn
Distributed by China International Book Trading Corporation
35 Chegongzhuang Xilu, Beijing 100044, China
P.O.Box 399, Beijing, China

Printed in the People's Republic of China

Contents

Acknowledgements

This is a newly revised edition of the *Dao De Jing* (*Tao-Te Ching*). It bears particular reference to the Mawangdui silk-copies and other old versions including those of Wang Bi and Heshang Gong, etc. What is most noteworthy herein are a number of textual rearrangements and modifications. All this is largely based on recent philological studies of the Daoist (Taoist) classic made by such leading Lao Zi (Lao-tzu) scholars as Gu Di, Zhou Ying, Chen Guying, Ren Jiyu, Gao Heng, Ma Xulun, Yan Lingfeng, Sha Shaohai and many others.

The contemplation of this task is considerably inspired by two most important works in Chinese: one is the *Lao Zi Tong* (A Systematic Revision of the *Dao*

De Jing) by Gu Di and ZhouYing, and the other is the *Lao Zi Zhuyi Ji Pingjie* (An Annotated and Paraphrased *Dao De Jing* with Commentary) by Chen Guying. They are virtually working encyclopedias of Lao Zi studies at the present stage. The English rendering of this edition owes a great deal to the existing translations by Chan Wing-tsit, Robert G. Henricks, He Guanghu et al.

I would like to take this occasion to acknowledge my gratitude to all these scholars aforementioned.

Preface

Lao Zi is considered the founder of early Daoism (Taoism) and studied worldwide. As has been observed by both oriental and occidental readers (e.g. Hegel), the ideas of Lao Zi tend to be more philosophical in the pure sense of this term when compared with those of his contemporaries in China. It is commonly acknowledged that Lao Zi's philosophizing is one of the main sources underlying the structure or formation of the overall psychology of the Chinese people.

Lao Zi's philosophizing is basically presented in the *Dao De Jing*, with such English renderings as *The Way and Its Power* or *Tao-Te Ching* (as a translitera-

on

tion of its non-standard Chinese pronunciation). This book, the major Daoist (Taoist) classic, is composed of 81 chapters as arranged by Heshang Gong. The classification itself remains all along controversial, even though it was once officially approved by an emperor of Tang Dynasty in 8th century. The compilation of the *Dao De Jing* by Heshang Gong features an additional subtitle for each chapter to help the reader approach the book in a more convenient and rewarding manner. This has conduced to my methodology of rearranging all the texts thematically in order to facilitate, I hope, a more practical or fruitful reading today (cf. Appendix). It has in turn given birth to this newly revised edition with relevant modifications.

Lao Zi, as a Daoist philosopher, is attracting more and more attention and interest both in the East and the West. Accordingly his book enjoys a rapidly increasing number of readers today. There are, consequently, more than a dozen of English versions of the *Dao De Jing* available published in various countries. The reason why we felt it important to add one more lies in the following considerations:

(1) 1973 witnessed the discovery of the Mawangdui silk copies of the *Dao De Jing*. According to relevant archaeological studies, one of the Mawangdui versions may date back at least to the third century BC, and is regarded as the oldest edition found so far (Note: The Guodian version on bamboo slips discovered in 1993 appears even older, but its content partly varies from the Mawangdui silk copies and it is assumed to be produced by a different author). It is therefore necessary to revise the previous texts with particular

reference to the Mawangdui findings.

(2) It is largely due to the favorable cultural policy introduced since China embarked on the reform policy in 1980s that the studies of Lao Zi and his like have made far more progress than ever before. But most of the latest achievements in this field are missing from the versions of the *Dao De Jing* available in English and other Western languages. This edition is intended to fill in this gap.

(3) Most of its English versions tend to employ the ready-made terms to translate the ideas of Lao Zi, which I find most likely to lead the reader onto the beaten track of the occidental cultural background when it comes to

cognizing what the author is supposed to say. In this case I have ventured to translate the key concepts with newly coined terminology. I sincerely hope that this approach will help the reader rethink from a new perspective, and better identify what is really meant, in line with textual and contextual analysis.

(4) Previously mentioned, this version of the *Dao De Jing* is thematically rearranged with attempts to facilitate a more practical and fruitful reading today. The thematic arrangement as such is based not merely on the scrutiny of Lao Zi's philosophizing as a systematic whole, but also on considerations of the reading habit of the English reader. The overall aim is to obtain a more relevant understanding and effective communication with regard to the text.

(5) The present approach to the *Dao De Jing* is largely grounded on the conviction that it will be of more advantages to have the reader di-

rectly involved in textual reading and analysis rather than to take a detour by tackling merely second-hand interpretation or reinterpretation. For it is often the case that an idiosyncratic interpreter, conceived of his own authority, gallops ahead while neglecting the reader's initiative and observation.

I must confess that whatever efforts I have to tackle this formidable project, it seems to me that I cannot hope to have succeeded completely. All too often the revision alone puts me under the impression that it is extremely difficult to transfer the thought of so lucid and poetic a writer as Lao Zi from one language to another without some damage occurring in the process. I found that the rhyming system, for instance, was almost untransferable no matter how hard I have tried. On the other hand, the *Dao De Jing* was written in a style based on metaphors and an expressive form of aphorisms such that many of the ideas presented appear to be engagingly suggestive, polysemous and somewhat ambiguous rather than articulate. Thus elaborate annotation and extended commentary are of need for the reader to attain a justified comprehension and interpretation, and fortunately there are some references of this kind available in English. *The Classic of the Dao* (1998), for instance, is one of them.

Incidentally, as regards the straightforward translation of the book, as many English renderings are, it seems to me as though a glass of fine wine has been mixed with water, reducing it to a less tasteful cocktail. But still it is of practical value for it serves to make inter-cultural communication or dialogue possible to certain extent.

In carrying out the actual work, I have been very fortunate to receive generous support from late Professor Herbert Mainusch of Münster University in Germany. I always cherish the memory of our obsessed conversations over the *Dao De Jing* during his stay in Beijing and my visit to Münster years ago.

Now Professor Albert A. Anderson is working

on a Mind Series in CD form. He has selected some classics by the most outstanding of all world thinkers. Among many others, the *Dao De Jing* is included and this very version in English is to be used. Such an academic venture by means of high-tech is sure to offer one more walking stick for those who are interested in exploring Lao Zi's thoughts.

Finally, I wish to extend my sincere thanks to my publisher and editor for their unflagging assistance when making this handy version.

Wang Keping
Beijing, China
Spring, 2008

Dao De Jing

【 Chapter 1 】

The *Dao* that can be told is not the constant *Dao*.

The Name that can be named is not the constant Name.

The Being-without-form is the origin of Heaven and Earth;

The Being-within-form is the mother of the myriad things.

Therefore it is always from the Being-without-form
That the subtlety of the *Dao* can be contemplated;
Similarly it is always from the Being-within-form
That the manifestation of the *Dao* can be perceived.
These two have the same source but different names,
They both may be called deep and profound.
The Deepest and most profound
Is the doorway to all subtleties.

【 Chapter 2 】

When the people of the world know the beautiful as beauty,

There arises the recognition of the ugly.

When they know the good as good,

There arises the recognition of the evil.

This is the reason why

Have-substance and have-no-substance produce each other;

Difficult and easy complete each other;

Long and short contrast with each other;

High and low are distinguished from each other;

Sound and voice harmonize with each other;

Front and back follow each other.

Thus, the sage conducts affairs through take-no-action;

He spreads his doctrines through wordless teaching;

He lets all things grow without his initiation;

He nurtures all things but takes possession of nothing;

He promotes all things but lays no claim to his ability;

He accomplishes his work but takes no credit for his contribution.

It is because he takes no credit

That his accomplishment stays with him for ever.

【 *Chapter 3* 】

Try not to exalt the worthy,

　So that people shall not compete.

Try not to value rare treasures,

　So that people shall not steal.

Try not to display the desirable,

　So that people's hearts shall not be disturbed.

Therefore the sage governs people by

　Purifying their minds,

　Filling their bellies,

　Weakening their ambitions,

　And strengthening their bones.

　He always keeps them innocent of knowledge and desires,

　And makes the crafty afraid to run risks.

　He conducts affairs on the principle of take-no-action,

　And everything will surely fall into order.

【 Chapter 4 】

The *Dao* is empty (like a bowl),

Its usefulness can never be exhausted.

The *Dao* is bottomless (like a valley),

Perhaps the ancestor of all things.

Invisible or formless, it appears non-existing

But actually it exists.

I don't know whose child it is at all.

It seems to have even preceded the Lord.

【 Chapter 5 】

Heaven and Earth are not humane.

They regard all things as straw dogs.

The sage is not humane.

He regards all people as straw dogs.

The space between Heaven and Earth isn't like a bellows?

While vacuous, it is never exhaustible.

When active, it turns out even more.

(To talk too much will surely lead to a quick demise.

Hence it is better to keep to tranquility.)

【 Chapter 6 】

The spirit of the valley is immortal.

It is called the subtle and profound female.

The gate of the subtle and profound female

 Is the root of Heaven and Earth.

It is continuous and everlasting,

With a utility never exhausted.

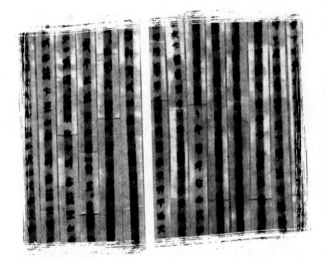

【 Chapter 7 】

Heaven is eternal and Earth everlasting.

They can be so just because they do not exist for themselves.

And for this reason they can long endure.

Therefore the sage places himself in the background,

But finds himself in the foreground.

He puts himself away without self-consideration,

And yet he always remains well-preserved.

It is because he has no personal interests

That his personal interests are fulfilled.

【 *Chapter 8* 】

The supreme good is like water.

Water is good at benefiting all things

And yet it does not compete with them.

It dwells in places that people detest,

And thus it is so close to the *Dao*.

In dwelling, (the best man) loves where it is low.

In the mind, he loves what is profound.

In dealing with others, he loves sincerity.

In speaking, he loves faithfulness.

In governing, he loves order.

In handling affairs, he loves competence.

In his activities, he loves timeliness.

Since he does not compete,

He is free from any fault.

【 Chapter 9 】

To talk too much will lead to a quick demise.

Hence, it is better to keep to tranquility.

To keep what is full from overflowing

Is not as good as to let it be.

If a sword-edge is sharpened to its sharpest,

It will not be able to last long.

When your rooms are filled with gold and jade,

You will not be able to keep them safe.

If you become arrogant because of honor and wealth,

It will bring upon you misfortune.

Retreat as soon as the work is done.

Such is the *Dao* of Heaven.

【 *Chapter 10* 】

Can you keep the spirit and embrace the One
  Without departing from them?
Can you concentrate your vital force and achieve
tenderness
  Like an infant without any desires?
Can you purify your mind and contemplate in
depth
  Without any flecks?
Can you love people and govern the state
  Without taking action?
Can you play the role of the feminine
  In the opening and closing of the gates of Heaven?
Can you understand and penetrate all things
  Without using your intelligence?

【 Chapter 11 】

Thirty spokes are united around the hub to make a
wheel,
But it is on the central hole for the axle
That the utility of the chariot depends.
Clay is kneaded to mold a utensil,
But it is on the empty space inside it
That the utility of the utensil depends.
Doors and windows are cut out to form a room,
But it is on the interior vacancy
That the utility of the room depends.
Therefore, have-substance brings advantage
While have-no-substance creates utility.

【 Chapter 12 】

The five colors make one's eyes blind.

The five tones make one's ears deaf.

The five flavors dull one's palate.

Racing and hunting unhinge one's mind.

Goods that are hard to get tempt people to rob and steal.

Hence, the sage cares for the belly instead of the eyes;

And he rejects the latter but accepts the former.

【 Chapter 13 】

One is alarmed when in receipt of favor or disgrace.

One has great trouble because of one's body that he has.

What is meant by being alarmed by favor or disgrace?

Favor is regarded as superior, and disgrace as inferior.

One is alarmed when one receives them

And equally alarmed when one loses them.

This is what is meant by being alarmed by favor or disgrace.

What is meant by having great trouble because of the body?

The reason why I have great trouble is that I have a body.

If I had no body,

What trouble could I have?

Hence he who values the world similarly as he values his body

Can be entrusted with the world.

He who loves the world in the same way as he loves his body

Can be entrusted with the world.

【 *Chapter 14* 】

You look at it but cannot see it;
 It is called the imageless.
You listen to it but cannot hear it;
 It is called the soundless.
You touch it but cannot find it;
 It is called the formless.
These three cannot be further inquired into,
 For they are the inseparable One.
The One is not bright when it is up,
 And not dark when it is down.
Infinite and indistinct, it cannot be named,
 Thus reverting to a state of non-thing-ness.
This is called shape without shape,
 Or image without image.
It is also called the Vague and the Elusive.
When meeting it, you cannot see its head,

When following it, you cannot see its back.

Hold on to the *Dao* of old in order to harness present things.

From this you may know the primeval beginning.

This is called the law of the *Dao*.

【 *Chapter 15* 】

He who was adept at practicing the *Dao* in antiquity

Was subtly profound and penetrating, too deep to be understood.

As he was beyond people's cognitive capacity,

I can only describe him arbitrarily:

He was cautious, as if walking across a frozen river in winter;

He was vigilant, as if being threatened by an attack on all sides;

He was solemn and reserved, like a visiting guest;

He was supple and pliant, like ice about to melt;

He was broad, like the boundless sea;

He was vigorous, like the untiring blowing wind;

He was genuine and plain, like an uncarved block;

He was open and expansive, like a great valley;

He was merged and indifferent, like muddy water.

Who could make the muddy gradually clear via tranquility?

Who could make the still gradually come to life via activity?

(It was nobody else but him.)

He who maintains the *Dao* does not want to be overflowing.

It is just because he does not want to be overflowing

That he can be renewed when worn out.

【 Chapter 16 】

Try the utmost to get the heart into complete vacuity.

Be sure to keep the mind in steadfast tranquility.

All things are growing and developing

And I see thereby their cycles.

Though all things flourish with a myriad of variations,

Each one eventually returns to its root.

This returning to its root is called tranquility;

This tranquility is called returning to its destiny;

Returning to its destiny is called the eternal.

To know the eternal is called enlightenment and wisdom.

Not to know the eternal is to take blind action,

Thus resulting in disaster.

He who knows the eternal can embrace all.

He who embraces all can be impartial.

He who is impartial can be all-encompassing.

He who is all-encompassing can be at one with Heaven.

He who is at one with Heaven can be at one with the *Dao*.

He who is at one with the *Dao* can be everlasting
And free from danger throughout his life.

老子

混元之祖太清之尊
五千言旨括乾坤

〖 *Chapter 17* 〗

The best kind of rulers are those whose existence

Is merely known by the people below them.

The next-best are those who are loved and praised.

The next-best are those who are feared.

The next-best are those who are despised.

If trust in others is not sufficient,

It will be unrequited.

(The best rulers) are cautious,

And seldom issue orders.

When tasks are accomplished and affairs completed,

The common people will say,

"We simply follow the way of spontaneity."

【 Chapter 18 】

When the great *Dao* is rejected,

Human-heartedness and righteousness will arise.

When knowledge and craftiness appear,

Great hypocrisy will emerge.

When the six family relations are not in harmony,

Filial piety and parental affection will be advocated.

When a country falls into chaos,

Loyal ministers will be praised.

【 Chapter 19 】

Only when sageness is eliminated and craftiness discarded,

Will people benefit a hundredfold.

Only when human-heartedness is eradicated and righteousness abandoned,

Will people return to filial piety and parental affection.

Only when skill is thrown away and profit ignored,

Will there be no more robbers or thieves.

Yet, these three are inadequate as a doctrine,

We therefore urge the following:

Manifest plainness and embrace simplicity;

Reduce selfishness and have few desires;

And get rid of learning and have no worries.

【 Chapter 20 】

How much difference is there between ready approval

And outright denunciation?

How much difference is there between good and evil?

What people fear cannot but be feared.

The multitude are merry, as if feasting on a day of sacrifice,

Or as if ascending a tower to enjoy the scenery in spring.

I alone remain tranquil and reluctant to distinguish.

I feel broad and far-reaching, as if at a loss.

I am indifferent and without concern,

Like an infant that cannot smile.

I am wearied indeed, as if I have no home to return to.

The multitude are so brilliant and self-exhibiting,

I alone seem to be lost in darkness and ignorance.

The multitude are so observant and discriminating,

I alone intend to make no distinction.

The multitude possess more than enough,

I alone seem to lack everything.

The multitude have their reason for taking action,

I alone seem to be clumsy and incapable of nothing.

The multitude like to be endorsed and supported,

I alone value the realization and attainment of the

Dao.

【 Chapter 21 】

The character of the great *De*
 Follows from the *Dao* alone.
What is called the *Dao*
 Appears elusive and vague.
Vague and elusive as it is,
 There is the image in it.
Elusive and vague as it is,
 There is the real in it.
Profound and obscure as it is,
There is the essence in it.
The essence is very concrete
 And contains the proof inside it.
From the present back to the past
 Its name continues to ever last,
 By which alone we may know the beginning of
all things.

How do I know their beginning as such?
Only through this.

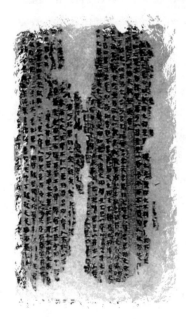

【 Chapter 22 】

To yield is yet to be preserved intact.

To be bent is yet to become straight.

To be hollow is yet to become full.

To be worn out is yet to be renewed.

To have little is yet to gain.

To have much is yet to be perplexed.

Therefore the sage holds on to the One

 And thus becomes a model for the world.

He does not cling to his ideas.

Therefore he is able to see things clearly.

He does not claim to be always right.

Therefore he is able to tell right from wrong.

He does not boast of himself.

Therefore he is given credit.

He does not think himself superior.

Therefore he is qualified for leadership.

It is only because he does not compete
 That the world cannot compete with him.
How could such an old saying be false
 As "To yield is yet to be preserved intact?"
Truly one will be preserved wholly
Without going to the contrary.
This is a constant and natural precept.

【 Chapter 23 】

A whirlwind does not last a whole morning;

A rainstorm does not last a whole day.

What causes them to be so?

It is Heaven and Earth.

If Heaven and Earth cannot make them last long,

 How much less can man?

Therefore, he who seeks the *Dao* is identified with it.

He who seeks the *De* is identified with it.

He who seeks Heaven is identified with it.

He who is identified with the *Dao*,

 The *Dao* is also happy to have him.

He who is identified with the *De*,

 The *De* is also happy to have him.

He who is identified with Heaven,

Heaven is also happy to have him.

◀ *Chapter 24* ▶

He who stands on tiptoe is not steady.

He who doubles his stride cannot go far.

He who displays himself is not wise.

He who justifies himself is not prominent.

He who boasts of himself is not given any credit.

He who feels self-important is not fit for leadership.

From the perspective of the *Dao*,

These are like remnants of food and tumors of the body,

So disgusting that one with the *Dao* stays away from them.

Likewise the sage knows himself but does not display himself.

He loves himself but does not feel self-important.

Hence, he rejects that and accepts this.

【 Chapter 25 】

There was something undifferentiated and all-embracing,

Which existed before Heaven and Earth.

Soundless and formless, it depends on nothing external

And stays inexhaustible.

It operates with a circular motion

And remains inextinguishable.

It may be considered the mother of all things under Heaven.

I do not know its name, and hence call it the *Dao* far-fetchedly.

If forced to give it another name, I shall call it the Great.

The Great is boundless and thus functioning everywhere.

It is functioning everywhere and thus becoming far-reaching.

It is becoming far-reaching and thus returning to the original point.

Therefore the *Dao* is great.

Heaven is great.

Earth is great.

And Man is also great.

There are four great things in the universe,

And Man is one of them.

Man follows the way of Earth.

Earth follows the way of Heaven.

Heaven follows the way of the *Dao*.

And the *Dao* follows the way of spontaneity.

【 Chapter 26 】

The heavy is the root of the light.

The tranquil is the lord of the hasty.

Therefore the sage travels all day

Without leaving behind his baggage cart.

Although he enjoys a magnificent and comfortable life,

He remains at leisure and without self-indulgence in it.

How is it that a king with ten thousand chariots

Governs his kingdom so lightly and hastily?

Lightness is sure to lose the root.

Hastiness is sure to lose the lord.

【 Chapter 27 】

He who is adept at traveling leaves no track or trace behind.

He who is adept at speaking makes no blemishes or flaws.

He who is adept at counting uses no tallies or counters.

He who is adept at shutting the door needs no bolts,
And yet it cannot be opened when shut.

He who is adept at binding things needs no strings,
And yet they cannot be untied when bound.

【 Chapter 28 】

He who knows the masculine and keeps to the feminine

 Will become the ravine of the world.

 Being the ravine of the world,

 He will never depart from the constant *De*,

 But return to the state of infancy.

 He who knows glory but keeps to disgrace

 Will become the valley of the world.

 Being the valley of the world,

 He will be proficient in the constant *De*

 And return to the state of simplicity.

 He who knows the white but keeps to the black

 Will become the principle of the world.

 Being the principle of the world,

 He will possess the constant *De*

 And return to the state of ultimate infinity.

(When simplicity is broken up,

It is turned into vessels.

By using these vessels,

The sage becomes the head of officials.

Hence a perfect government is not carved out of
artificiality.)

【 Chapter 29 】

I think that a person will not succeed

When he desires to govern the state and act upon it.

The state as a sacred vessel should not be acted upon,

Nor should it be held on to.

He who acts upon it will harm it.

He who holds on to it will lose it.

Thus the sage takes no action, and therefore fails in nothing;

He holds on to nothing, and therefore loses nothing.

Of all the creatures some lead and some follow;

Some breathe and some blow;

Some are strong and some are weak;

Some rise up and some fall down.

Hence the sage discards the extreme,

The extravagant and the excessive.

Meanwhile, he desires to have no desires.

He does not value rare treasures.

He learns what is unlearned.

He returns to what is missed.

Thus he helps all things in natural development,

But does not dare to take any action.

【 Chapter 30 】

He who assists the ruler with the *Dao*

Never seeks to dominate the world with military force.

The use of force is intrinsically dangerous:

Wherever armies are stationed,

Briers and thorns grow wild.

As soon as great wars are over,

Years of famine are sure to afflict the land.

Therefore an adept commander (of a defensive force) will

Stop when he has achieved his aim.

He does not use force to dominate the world.

He achieves his aim but does not become arrogant.

He achieves his aim but does not boast about it.

He achieves his aim only because he has no other choice.

This is called achieving the aim without using force to dominate.

The strong and powerful rob and harm the old and weak.

This is called contrary to the *Dao*.

Whatever is contrary to the *Dao* will soon perish.

【 Chapter 31 】

Weapons are nothing but instruments of evil.

They are used only when there is no other choice.

Therefore, he who wins a battle is not praiseworthy.

If he thinks himself praiseworthy,

He delights in the victory.

He who delights in the victory

Delights in the slaughter of men.

He who delights in the slaughter of men

Will not succeed under Heaven.

For the multitude killed in the war

Let us mourn them with sorrow and grief.

For the victory won by force,

Let us observe the occasion with funeral ceremonies.

【 *Chapter 32* 】

The *Dao* is eternal and has no name.

Though it is simple and seems minute,

Nothing under Heaven can subordinate it.

If kings and lords were able to maintain it,

All people would submit spontaneously to them.

Heaven and Earth unite to drip sweet dew,

Without the command of men, it drips evenly over all.

Once a system comes into being,

Names are instituted.

Once names are instituted,

One has to know where and when to stop.

It is by knowing where and when to stop

That one can be free from danger.

Everything under Heaven is embraced by the *Dao*,

Just like every river or stream running into the sea.

【 Chapter 33 】

He who knows others is knowledgeable.

He who knows himself is wise.

He who conquers others is physically strong.

He who conquers himself is mighty.

He who is contented is rich.

He who acts with persistence has will.

He who does not lose his place will endure.

He who dies but is not forgotten enjoys a long life.

【 *Chapter 34* 】

The great *Dao* flows everywhere.
It may go left or right.
All things rely on it for existence,
And never does it turn away from them.
When it accomplishes its work,
It does not claim credit for itself.
It preserves and nourishes all things,
But it does not claim to be master over them.
Thus it may be called the minute.
All things come to it as to their home,
Yet it does not act as their master.
Hence it may be called the great.
This is always the case with the sage
Who is able to achieve his greatness
Just because he himself never strives to be great.

【 Chapter 35 】

If you hold fast to the great image,
All the people under Heaven will come to you.
They will come and do no harm to each other,
But will all enjoy comfort, peace and health.
Music and dainties can make passers-by tarry,
While the *Dao*, if spoken out, is insipid and tasteless.
Being looked at, it is imperceptible.
Being listened to, it is inaudible.
Being utilized, it is inexhaustible.

【 *Chapter 36* 】

In order to contract it,

It is necessary to expand it first.

In order to weaken it,

It is necessary to strengthen it first.

In order to destroy it,

It is necessary to promote it first.

In order to grasp it,

It is necessary to offer it first.

This is called subtle light.

The soft and the tender overcome the hard and the strong.

(Just as) fish should not be taken away from deep water,

The sharp weapons of the state should not be displayed to its people.

【 Chapter 37 】

The *Dao* invariably takes no action,

And yet there is nothing left undone.

If kings and lords are able to maintain it,

All things will submit to them due to self-transformation.

If, after submission, they have resurging desires to act,

I should subdue them by the nameless simplicity.

When they are subdued by the nameless simplicity,

They will be free of desires.

Being free of desires, they will be tranquil,

And the world will of itself be rectified.

見聽之不足聞用之不可既

將欲歙之必固張之將欲弱

之必固強之將欲廢之必固

興之將欲奪之必固與之

是謂微明柔弱勝剛強

魚不可脫於淵國之利器

不可以示人

道常無為而無不為侯王

若能守萬物將自化化而

欲作吾將鎮之以無名之樸

無名之樸亦將不欲不欲以

靜天下將自正

老子道經卷上

【 Chapter 38 】

The man of the superior *De* is not conscious of it,

And in this way he really possesses it.

The man of the inferior *De* never loses sight of it,

And in this way he really has none of it.

The man of the superior *De* takes no action

And thus nothing will be left undone.

The man of the inferior *De* takes action

And thus something will be left undone.

The man of superior human-heartedness takes action

And so acts without purpose.

The man of superior righteousness takes action

And so acts on purpose.

The man of superior propriety takes action,

And when people do not respond to it,

He will stretch out his arms and force them to

comply.

Therefore, only when the *Dao* is lost does the *De* disappear.

Only when the *De* is lost does human-heartedness appear.

Only when human-heartedness is lost does righteousness appear.

Only when righteousness is lost does propriety appear.

Now propriety is a superficial expression of loyalty and

Faithfulness, and the beginning of disorder.

The man of foreknowledge has but the flower of the *Dao*,

And this is the beginning of ignorance.

Hence the great man dwells in the thick instead of the thin.

He dwells in the fruit instead of the flower.

Therefore he rejects the latter and accepts the former.

老子
著之道德
五千言而去
藥不之儔
不言白日
昇青天
壽者歟

【 *Chapter 39* 】

Of those in the past that obtained the One:

Heaven obtained the One and became clear;

The earth obtained the One and became tranquil;

The Gods obtained the One and became divine;

The valleys obtained the One and became full;

All things obtained the One and became alive and
kept growing;

Kings and lords obtained the One and the world
became peaceful.

Taking this to its logical conclusion we may say:

If Heaven had not thus become clear,

It would soon have cracked;

If the earth had not thus become tranquil,

It would soon have broken apart;

If the Gods had not thus become divine,

They would soon have perished;

If the valleys had not thus become full,

They would soon have dried up;

If all things had not thus become alive and kept growing,

They would soon have become extinct;

If kings and lords had not thus become honorable and noble,

They would soon have toppled and fallen.

It is always the case

That the noble takes the humble as its root.

And the high takes the low as its base.

Hence kings and lords call themselves

The orphaned, the solitary or the unworthy.

This is regarding the humble as the root of the noble, is it not?

People disdain the "orphaned," "solitary" or "unworthy."

And yet kings and lords call themselves by these terms.

Therefore the highest honor needs no flattering.

Thus with everything-

Sometimes it may increase when decreased,

And sometimes it may decrease when increased.

For this reason —

They desire not to dazzle and glitter like jade,

But to remain firm and plain like stone.

【 Chapter 40 】

Reversion is the movement of the *Dao*.

Weakness is the function of the *Dao*.

All things under Heaven come from Being-within-form.

And Being-within-form comes from Being-without-form.

【 Chapter 41 】

When the highest type of literati hear of the *Dao*,
  They diligently practice it.
When the average type of literati hear of the *Dao*,
They half-believe it.
When the lowest type of literati hear of the *Dao*,
They laugh heartily at it.
If they did not laugh at it, it would not be the *Dao*.
Therefore, there are such established sayings:
The *Dao* that is bright seems to be dark;
The *Dao* that advances seems to retreat;
The *Dao* that is level seems to be uneven.
Thus the great *De* appears empty like a valley;
The far-reaching *De* appears insufficient;
The vigorous *De* appears inert;
The simplistic *De* appears clumsy;
The whitest appears soiled;

The greatest square has no corners;

The greatest vessel is unfinished;

The greatest music sounds faint;

The greatest form has no shape;

The *Dao* is hidden and nameless.

Yet it is the *Dao* that initiates all things

And brings them to completion.

【 Chapter 42 】

The *Dao* produces the One.

The One turns into the Two.

The Two give rise to the Three.

The Three bring forth the myriad of things.

The myriad things contain the *Yin* and the *Yang* as vital forces,

Which achieve harmony through their interactions.

【 Chapter 43 】

The softest thing in the world

Runs in and out of the hardest thing.

The invisible force penetrates any creviceless being.

Thereby I come to know the advantage of take-no-action.

Few in the world can realize the merits of wordless teaching

And the benefits of doing nothing.

【 Chapter 44 】

Which is more dear, fame or life?

Which is more valuable, life or wealth?

Which is more detrimental, gain or loss?

Thus an excessive love of fame

Is bound to cause an extravagant expense.

A rich hoard of wealth

Is bound to suffer a heavy loss.

Therefore he who is contented will encounter no disgrace.

He who knows when and where to stop will meet no danger.

And in this way he can endure longer.

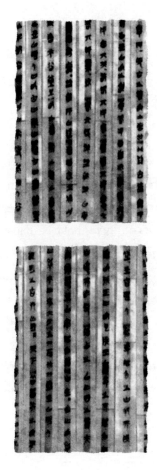

80

【 Chapter 45 】

What is most perfect seems to be incomplete,

But its utility cannot be impaired.

What is most full seems to be empty,

But its utility cannot be exhausted.

The most straight seems to be crooked.

The greatest skill seems to be clumsy.

The greatest eloquence seems to stutter.

The tranquil overcomes the hasty.

The cold overcomes the hot.

By remaining quiet and tranquil,

One can become a model for all the people.

【 *Chapter 46* 】

When the world has the *Dao*,

War horses are used in farming.

When the world lacks the *Dao*,

Even mares in foal have to serve in battle.

There is no guilt greater than lavish desires.

There is no calamity greater than discontentment.

There is no defect greater than covetousness.

Therefore, he who is contented with knowing contentment

Is always contented indeed.

【 Chapter 47 】

Without going out of the door
One may know the all under the sky.
Without looking through the window
One may see the *Dao* of Heaven.
The further one goes,
The less one knows.
Therefore the sage knows without going about,
Understands without sense perception,
And accomplishes without taking action.

【 Chapter 48 】

The pursuit of learning is to increase day after day.
The pursuit of the *Dao* is to decrease day after day.
It decreases and decreases again
Till one gets to the point of take-no-action.
He takes no action and yet nothing is left undone.
In order to govern all under Heaven
One should adopt the policy of doing nothing.
A person who likes to do anything arbitrary,
Is not qualified to govern all under Heaven.

【 Chapter 49 】

The sage has no fixed mind of his own.

He takes the mind of the populace as his mind.

I treat those who are good with goodness

And I also treat those who are not good with goodness,

Then everyone will try to become good.

I trust those who are trustworthy

And I also trust those who are not trustworthy,

Then everyone will try to become trustworthy.

When the sage governs the world,

He seeks to put away his personal will

And to help everyone return to the sphere of simplicity.

While the people all concentrate on their own eyes and ears,

He renders them back to the sphere of infancy without desires.

【 Chapter 50 】

Man comes alive into the world

And goes dead into the earth.

Three out of ten will live longer.

Three out of ten will live shorter.

And three out of ten will strive for long life

But meet premature death.

And for what reason?

It is because of excessive life-preservation.

Only those who don't value their lives are wiser

Than those who overvalue their lives.

I have heard that those who are good at preserving life

Will not meet rhinoceroses or tigers when traveling the byways,

And will not be wounded or killed when fighting battles.

The rhinoceroses cannot butt their horns against them.

The tigers cannot fasten their claws upon them.

And weapons cannot thrust their blades into them.

And for what reason?

Because they are out of the range of death.

【 Chapter 51 】

The *Dao* begets all beings,

And the *De* fosters them.

Substance gives them physical forms,

And environment completes them.

Therefore all beings venerate the *Dao* and honor the *De*.

As for the veneration of the *Dao* and the honoring of the *De*,

It is not out of obedience to any orders;

It comes spontaneously due to their naturalness.

Hence the *Dao* begets all beings,

And the *De* fosters them,

Rears them and develops them,

Matures them and makes them bear fruit,

Protects them and helps them breed.

To produce them without taking possession of

them,

To raise them without vaunting this as its own merit,

And to nourish them without controlling them,

This is called the Profound *De*.

【 Chapter 52 】

There was a beginning of the universe,

Which may be called the mother of the universe.

He who has found the mother

Thereby understands her sons;

He who has understood the sons

And still keeps to the mother

Will be free from danger throughout his life.

Block up the holes;

Shut up the doors;

And till the end of life there will be no toil.

Open the holes;

Meddle with affairs;

And till the end of life there will be no salvation.

Seeing what is small is called enlightenment.

Keeping to weakness is called strength.

Use the light.

Revert to enlightenment.

And thereby avoid danger to one's life-

This is called practicing the eternal.

【 Chapter 53 】

If I have a little wisdom,

I will walk along a broad way

And fear nothing but going astray.

The broad way is very even,

But the powerful delight in by-paths.

The courts are exceedingly corrupt,

Whereas the fields are exceedingly weedy

And the granaries are exceedingly empty.

They are wearing elegant clothes,

Carrying sharp swords,

Enjoying exquisite food and drink,

And owning abundant wealth and treasures.

They can be called robber chieftains.

This is surely against the *Dao*.

【 Chapter 54 】

He who is good at building cannot be shaken.

He who is good at holding can lose nothing.

Thus his ancestral sacrifice can pass down

From generation to generation.

When cultivated and exercised in the person,

The *De* will become pure and genuine.

When cultivated and exercised in the family,

The *De* will become full and overflowing.

When cultivated and exercised in the community,

The *De* will become constant and everlasting.

When cultivated and exercised nationwide,

The *De* will become powerful and abundant.

When cultivated and exercised worldwide,

The *De* will become universal and widespread.

Therefore, (by taking it as a standard we should)

Use this person to examine other persons,

Use this family to examine other families,

Use this community to examine other communities,

Use this country to examine other countries,

And use this world to examine other worlds.

How do I know the situation of all things under Heaven?

Precisely by the method above-mentioned.

【 Chapter 55 】

He who possesses the *De* in abundance

Can be compared to a newborn infant.

Poisonous insects will not sting him.

Fierce brutes will not injure him.

Birds of prey will not attack him.

His bones are weak and his sinews tender,

But his grasp is firm.

He does not yet know about the intercourse of male and female,

But his organ is aroused,

For his physical essence is at its height.

He may cry all day without becoming hoarse,

For his innate harmony is simply perfect.

The essence and harmony as such are natural and constant.

To know this is called being wise.

The desire to multiply life's enjoyments means ill omen.

The mind to employ vital energy excessively means fatal stiffness.

Things that have grown strong commence to become old.

This is called "being contrary to the *Dao*."

Whatever is contrary to the *Dao* will soon perish.

【 Chapter 56 】

He who knows does not speak,

He who speaks does not know.

He blocks the vent,

Closes the door,

Blunts the sharpness,

Unties the tangles,

Softens the glare,

And mixes with the dust.

This is called the Profound Identification.

Therefore people cannot get intimate with him,

Nor can they estrange themselves from him.

People cannot benefit him,

Nor can they harm him.

People cannot ennoble him,

Nor can they debase him.

For this reason he is esteemed by all under the sky.

【 Chapter 57 】

A state should be governed in a normal way.

An army should be operated in an unusual way.

The world should be administered by doing nothing.

How do I know that it should be so?

Through the following:

The more prohibitive enactments there are in the world,

The poorer the people will become;

The more sharp weapons men have,

The more troubled the state will be;

The more crafts and techniques men possess,

The more vicious things will appear;

The more laws and orders are made prominent,

The more robbers and thieves will spring up.

Therefore the sage says:

"I take no action and people of themselves become transformed.

I love tranquility and people of themselves become righteous.

I disturb nobody and people of themselves become prosperous.

I have no desires and people of themselves become simple."

【 Chapter 58 】

When the government is generous and non-discriminatory,

    The people will remain honest and sincere;

    When the government is severe and discriminatory,

    The people will become crafty and cunning.

    Misfortune is that beside which fortune lies;

    Fortune is that beneath which misfortune lurks.

    Who knows what may be their ultimate cause?

    There is no fixed and normal frame of reference.

    The normal can suddenly turn into the abnormal,

    The good can suddenly turn into the evil.

    The people have been deluded for a long time.

Therefore, the sage is as pointed as a square, but never stays stiff;

    He is as sharp as a knife, but never cuts anybody;

He is frank and straightforward, but never aggressive;

He is bright and shining, but never dazzling.

【 Chapter 59 】

To rule people and to serve Heaven

Nothing is better than the principle of frugality.

Only by frugality can one get ready early.

To get ready early means to accumulate the *De* continuously.

With the continuous accumulation of the *De*,

One can overcome every difficulty.

If one can overcome every difficulty,

He will then acquire immeasurable capacity.

With immeasurable capacity,

He can achieve the *Dao* to govern the country.

He who has the *Dao* of the country can maintain sovereignty.

This is called the way in which the roots are planted deep

And the stalks are made firm.

Hence longevity is achieved

And sovereignty is made everlasting.

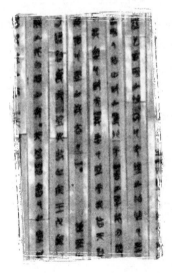

【 Chapter 60 】

Governing a large country is like cooking a small fish.

If the *Dao* is applied to the world,

Ghosts will lose their supernatural influence.

It is not that they will actually lose it,

But that their influence will no longer be able to harm men.

It is not that their influence will no longer be able to harm men,

But that the sage also will not harm men.

Since these two do not harm men, and vice versa,

They all enjoy peaceful co-existence.

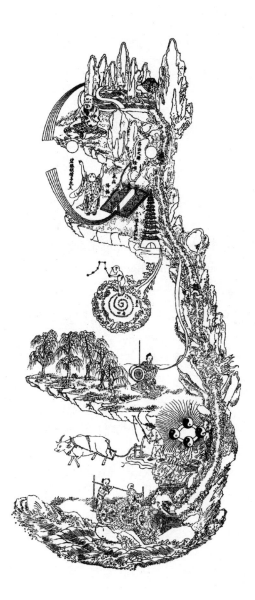

【 *Chapter 61* 】

Governing a large country is like lying in a lower place.

This country in the world may be likened to

Rivers and streams flowing into the sea.

It lies lower such that all in the world runs to it.

It is the converging point of all in the world.

It is the female of the world.

The female always overcomes the male via tranquility,

And with tranquility she lies lower.

Hence a big state can rally small states around it

If it lowers itself to them.

Small states can win trust from a big state

If they lower themselves to it.

Thus a big state can rally small states by lowering itself,

And small states can win trust from a big state by doing the same.

What a big state wants is to unite and lead small states.

What small states want is to be rallied and protected by the big state.

When both sides get what they respectively want,

The big state should learn to keep itself lower.

【 Chapter 62 】

The *Dao* is the storehouse of all things.

It is treasured by the good man,

And also preserved by the bad man.

Honored words can gain respect from others.

Fine deeds can have an impact on others.

Even if a man is bad,

Why should he be ever rejected?

Therefore, the sage is always good at saving men,

And consequently nobody is rejected.

He is always good at saving things,

And consequently nothing is rejected.

This is called the Hidden Light.

Therefore, the good man is the teacher of the bad man.

And the bad man is the material from which the good man may learn.

He who does not value the teacher or care for the material,

Will still be greatly deluded

Though he thinks himself intelligent.

Such is called the significant subtlety of the *Dao*.

Therefore, on the occasion of enthroning an emperor

Or installing the three ministers,

It is better to offer the *Dao* as a present

Though there are grand ceremonies of saluting them

With the round jadeware, followed by the four-horse chariot.

Why did the ancients value this *Dao* so much?

Did they not say, "Those who seek shall attain

And those who sin shall be freed?"

For this reason it is valued by all under Heaven.

【 Chapter 63 】

Consider take-no-action as a code of conduct.

Consider make-no-trouble as a way of deed.

Consider have-no-flavor as a method of taste.

It is a rule in the world that

The most difficult things begin with the easy,

And the largest things arise from the minute.

Hence, tackle the difficult while it is still easy;

Achieve the large while it is still minute.

For this reason, the sage never strives for the great,

And thereby he can accomplish it.

He who makes promises too readily will surely lack credibility.

He who takes things too easily will surely encounter difficulty.

Therefore, even the sage regards things as difficult,

And he is free from any difficulty as a result.

【 Chapter 64 】

What is stable is easy to hold.

What is not yet manifest is easy to handle.

What is brittle is easy to disintegrate.

What is minute is easy to eliminate.

Deal with matters before they occur.

Put them in order before disorder arises.

A tree as huge as one's embrace grows from a tiny shoot.

A tower of nine stories rises up from a heap of earth.

A journey of a thousand miles starts from the first step.

People often fail when they are on the point of success

In the process of conducting affairs.

If they remain still as careful at the end as at the beginning,

They will never suffer from failures.

【 *Chapter 65* 】

In ancient times he who practiced the *Dao* well

Did not use it to enlighten other people.

Instead he used it to make them simple.

Now people are difficult to govern

Because they have too much craftiness.

Thus, governing a country by craftiness is a disaster for it.

And not governing it by craftiness is a blessing for it.

He who knows these two also knows the principle.

It is called the Profound *De* to always know the principle.

The Profound *De* is deep and far-reaching;

It returns to the origin with all things,

And then leads to the great naturalness.

【 Chapter 66 】

Great rivers and seas can be kings of mountain streams

Because they skillfully stay below them.

That is why they can be their kings.

Therefore, in order to be above others,

The sage must place himself below them in his words.

In order to be ahead of others,

He must place himself behind them in his person.

In this way, the sage is above others,

But they do not feel his weight.

He is ahead of others,

But they do not feel his hindrance.

Therefore the whole world delights in praising him

And never grows tired of him.

Simply because he does not compete with others,

Nobody under Heaven can compete with him.

【 *Chapter 67* 】

I have three treasures that I grasp and keep.

The first is "kindness."

The second is "frugality."

The third is "not daring to be ahead of the world."

With kindness, one can become courageous.

With frugality, one can become generous.

With not daring to be ahead of the world,

One can become the leader of the world.

Now it is a fatal mistake

To seek courage by abandoning kindness,

To seek generosity by abandoning frugality,

And to seek precedence by abandoning retreat.

With kindness, one can be victorious in the case of attack,

And remain firm in the case of defence.

Heaven will help and protect such a one through kindness.

【 Chapter 68 】

In the past —

An adept commander did not display his martial prowess.

An adept warrior did not become angry.

An adept conqueror did not tussle with his enemy.

An adept manager of men placed himself below them.

This is called the virtue of non-competition.

This is called the use of others' force.

This is called the supreme principle of matching Heaven.

【 *Chapter 69* 】

In the past, a military strategist said:

"I dare not take the offensive, but I take the defensive.

I dare not advance an inch, but I retreat a foot."

This means (to make the invading force):

Advancing onward without battle formation,

Raising arms without morale enhancing,

Holding weapons not at the ready,

And tackling the foe without vis-à-vis fighting.

There is no greater disaster than underestimating the enemy.

Such underestimation is tantamount to self-abandonment.

Therefore, when two well-matched armies clash in battle

It is the side that retreats first that will win last.

【 *Chapter 70* 】

All the world says that my *Dao* is great,

But it does not resemble anything concrete.

Just because it is great,

It does not resemble anything concrete.

It would have been small for long if it did.

My words are very easy to understand and practice.

But no one in the world can understand and practice them.

My words have their own source,

My deeds have their own master.

It is merely because people do not know this

That they fail to understand me.

Those who can understand me are very few,

And those who can follow me are hard to meet.

Therefore the sage wears coarse garb

But conceals a precious jade in his bosom.

【 Chapter 71 】

It is all the best to know that you don't know.

It is an aberration to pretend to know when you don't know.

The sage is free from the aberration

Because he recognizes it as it is.

He can be free from this aberration

Only when he recognizes it as it is.

【 Chapter 72 】

When people do not fear the power of the ruler,
Something dreadful is liable to occur.
Do not force people out of their dwellings.
Do not exploit people to the point that they cannot
live.

They will not detest and overthrow the regime
Only when they are not excessively oppressed.

【 *Chapter 73* 】

He who is brave in daring will be killed.

He who is brave in not daring will survive.

Of these two kinds of bravery,

One is advantageous, while the other is harmful.

Heaven detests what it detests.

Who knows what could be its cause?

The *Dao* of Heaven does not compete, and yet it is good at winning.

It does not speak, and yet it is good at responding.

It is not called, and yet it comes along on its own.

It is frankly at ease, and yet it plans well.

The net of Heaven is large and vast,

It lets nothing escape, despite its wide meshes.

【 Chapter 74 】

If the people are not afraid of death,

What is the point of trying to frighten them with death?

In order to make people always afraid of death,

We can catch and kill the trouble-makers.

Then, who will dare to make trouble?

There is always a master in charge of executions.

To carry out executions in place of the master

Is like hewing wood in place of a skillful carpenter.

Of those who hew wood in place of the carpenter,

Very few can escape cutting their own finger.

【 *Chapter 75* 】

The people suffer from famine
Because the ruler levies too much tax-grain.
Thus they suffer from famine.
The people are difficult to rule
Because the ruler too often takes action.
Thus they are difficult to rule.
The people take life lightly
Because the ruler longs for life so avidly.
Thus they take life lightly.

【 Chapter 76 】

When alive, man is soft and tender.

After death, he is hard and stiff.

All things like grass and trees are soft and tender when alive,

Whereas they become withered and dried when dead.

Therefore, the hard and stiff are companions of death

Whereas the soft and tender are companions of life.

Hence an army will be shattered when it becomes strong.

A tree will be broken when it grows huge.

The hard and strong fall in the inferior position;

The soft and tender stay in the superior position.

"The violent and strong do not die natural deaths."

I shall take this principle as the father of my teaching.

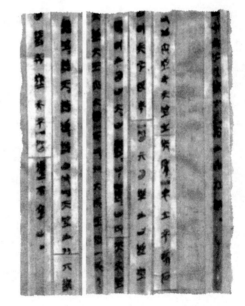

【 Chapter 77 】

Does not the *Dao* of Heaven resemble the drawing of a bow?

When the string is taut, press it down.

When it is low, raise it up.

When it is excessive, reduce it.

When it is insufficient, supplement it.

The *Dao* of Heaven reduces whatever is excessive

And supplements whatever is insufficient.

The *Dao* of man does the very opposite.

It reduces the insufficient

And adds more to the excessive.

Who is able to have a surplus to offer to the world?

Only the one who has the *Dao*.

The sage does not accumulate for himself.

The more he shares with others, the more he possesses.

The more he gives to others, the richer he becomes.

The *Dao* of Heaven benefits all things and causes no harm.

The *Dao* of the sage acts for others but never competes with them.

【 Chapter 78 】

Nothing in the world is softer and weaker than water,

But no force can compare with it in attacking the hard and strong.

For this reason there is no substitute for it.

Everyone in the world knows that

The soft can overcome the hard,

And the weak can overcome the strong,

But none can put it into practice.

Therefore the sage says:

"He who shoulders the disgrace for his nation

Can be the sovereign of the country;

He who bears the misfortune of his nation

Can be the king of the world."

Positive words seem to be their opposite.

【 *Chapter 79* 】

To reconcile two sides in deep hatred

Is surely to leave some hatred behind.

If one returns good for evil,

How can this be taken as a proper solution?

Therefore the sage keeps the counterfoil of the tally,

Yet he does not demand repayment of the debt.

The virtuous man is as kind and generous as the
tally keeper

But the non-virtuous is as harsh and calculating as
a tax collector.

The *Dao* of Heaven has no preference.

It is constantly with the good man.

【 *Chapter 80* 】

Let there be a small state with few people.

It has various kinds of instruments,

But let none of them be used.

Let the people there not risk their lives,

And not migrate far away.

Although they have boats and carriages,

Let there be no occasion to ride in them.

Although they have armor and weapons,

Let there be no occasion to display them.

Let the people return to knotting cords and using them.

Let them relish their food,

Beautify their clothing,

Feel comfortable in their homes

And delight in their customs.

Although the neighboring states are within the sight

of one another,

>And the crowing of cocks and barking of dogs

>On both sides can be heard,

>Their peoples may die of old age without ever fighting

each other.

【 Chapter 81 】

True words are not beautiful;

Beautiful words are not true.

A good man is not an eloquent arguer;

An eloquent arguer is not a good man.

He who knows does not show off his extensive
learning;

He who shows off his extensive learning does not
know.

Appendix:
A Thematic Reading Guide

1. The Essence of the *Dao*

The exposition of the *Dao* reveals Lao Zi's doctrine of the origin and coming into being of the universe on the one hand, and his philosophy of "following the way of spontaneity" on the other. The *You* (Being-within-form) and The *Wu* (Being-without-form) are described as the two essential aspects of the *Dao* from which its subtlety, profundity and dynamic potency can be discerned and perceived accordingly. The nature of the *Dao* is a topic that runs throughout the text of the *Dao De Jing* (DDJ), particularly in chapters 1, 4, 6 and 25 (DDJ).

2. The Features of the *Dao*

Lao Zi's concept of the *Dao* serves as the keystone for his philosophy in general, and the starting point for his doctrine of the origin of the universe in particular. With high awareness of the duality of the *Dao*, known as the *You* (Being-within-form) and the *Wu* (Being-without-form), Lao Zi exposes such general features as the *Dao*'s imagelessness, soundlessness, formlessness, vagueness and elusiveness with regard to "the inseparable One" (i.e. the *Dao*) and their interactions with their counterparts. This theme is focused in chapters 14, 35, 21 and 5 (DDJ).

3. The Movement of the *Dao*

The motion of the *Dao* is reckoned as having a dialectical character that reflects the growth, change and

decline of all things in a developmental cycle. The idea associated with "reversion" (*fan*), if not absolutized as it is by Lao Zi, can still have a valid message even judged from a modern perspective. Take a close look at Chapter 40 (DDJ).

4. The *Dao* and the Myriad Things

Lao Zi holds the view that the *Dao* is the omni-principle of all individual principles. Thus the *Dao* produces all things; and likewise all things develop from the *Dao*. The interactions and interrelations between the *Dao* and the myriad things are in fact the extension of his theory about the ultimate origin and coming into being of the universe, the process of which is historically significant due to its connection with the way of thought and world view of the ancient Chinese. And the function of the *Dao* in general can still find its traces and influences deep in the psycho-cultural structure of the Chinese people today. Go on to read chapters 42, 32, 34, and 39 (DDJ).

5. The *Dao* of Heaven and the *Dao* of Man

The distinction between the *Dao* of Heaven and the

Dao of man is set out in striking contrast. The former demonstrates itself as a symbol of naturalness, selflessness and equality in a virtuous sense, according to Lao Zi. It is therefore viewed as a measurement or frame of reference for the latter. The respective services and differences of the two are basically reflected in chapters 77 and 79 (DDJ).

6. From the *Dao* into the *De*

Both the *Dao* and the *De* have a variety of interpretations, which are presented in pairs. They include, for example, the Way and its Power, the Way and its Potency, the Way and the Walk on the Way, the all-embracing first principle for all things and the principle underlying each individual thing, the omni-determinant of all beings and its manifestation, etc. No matter what they may be, there is an interaction between them and a transformation from one into the other. This topic is explored with particular reference to chapters 51 and 38 (DDJ).

7. The Qualities of the *De*

The *De* functions in various domains due to its diversity of qualities. Similarly, it is cultivated and manifested in different ways, which all accord with the criteria of the *Dao*. The figurative depiction of the profundity of the *De* as an innocent infant is a rich contribution to one's understanding of the effects of the *De*. In this regard, chapters 54 and 55 (DDJ) deserve more attention.

8. On Have-substance and Have-no-substance

Distinct from "Being-within-form" and "Being-without-form," as defined in Chapter 1 (DDJ), "Have-substance" and "Have-no-substance" as a pair of concepts reflect Lao Zi's dialectical thinking in terms of their interaction and complementary relations. Lao Zi seems to infuse more importance into "Have-no-substance" (which means here "the empty space" or "non-existence" in a physical sense such as the vacancy inside a room, the space inside a utensil or the holes between the spokes of a wheel, etc.) since he believes it is more decisive in the aspects of utility and function. This

道可道非常道无名天地始

名万物之母故常無欲以观

其妙常有欲以观

is consistent with his general principle that "Being-within-form comes from Being-without-form" on the one hand, and his idea of "vacuity" (*xu*) for its receptivity and accommodability on the other. A textual analysis of Chapter 11 serves to illustrate the interrelations between "Have-substance" and "Have-no-substance".

9. On Take-action and Take-no-action

Take-no-action (*wuwei*) is one of the essential features of the *Dao*. It is virtually a substitute expression for "follow spontaneity" or "the way of naturalness." It is therefore recommended by Lao Zi as an ideal for political and governmental praxis since it facilitates the proper outcome of everything. Conversely, take-action (*youwei*), as an opposite solution, can be misleading and hindering owing to its imposition of purposefulness and limited capacity. In this connection one needs to look into chapters 37 and 29 (DDJ).

10. On Pleasure-snobbery and Acquisitiveness

It seems to be paradoxical that the progression of

civilization tends to bring forth advantages and disadvantages at the same time. The situation was more or less the same in the past. Lao Zi persistently focuses on the negative aspects of civilization in view of social ills. Based on his observation and anatomy of problematic reality in his time, his exposure of pleasure-snobbery and acquisitiveness sheds much light on the human condition even today. See chapters 12, 53 and 67 (DDJ).

11. On the Hard and the Soft

It seems to be a universal rule that the strong conquer the weak, and that the hard overwhelm the soft. However, Lao Zi thinks in reverse, say, from a dynamic and dialectical perspective. He grounds his philosophy of keeping to the soft and tender upon his empirical observation of natural changes. Plain and simplistic as his thinking may be, his method of reverse speculation remains fairly instructive even today. Chapters 43, 76 and 78 (DDJ) are the focus of this.

12. On the Beautiful and the Ugly

As regards the distinction between the beautiful and

the ugly, Lao Zi's treatise is characterized by relativity and mutualism. This is based on his observation that there are always two opposites in everything under the sky. These two opposites contrast and complete each other. Thus one cannot do without the other due to their mutuality and, likewise, one cannot exist without the other either. Make particular reference to Chapter 2 (DDJ).

13. On Beauty, Truth and Goodness

Lao Zi's exposition of beauty, truth and goodness features his dialectical thinking and skeptical perspective. His insight into the contradictions among the three values is penetrating, and his critique of the pretentiousness and artificiality is still enlightening even today. The unity of the three values seems to Lao Zi to be only possible in the *Dao* and not in a society imbued with craftiness and deception. Try to examine chapters 81 and 62 (DDJ).

14. On Modesty and Retreat

Modesty as a virtue has all along been appreciated

and recommended in the history of Chinese thought and ethics. It is not only practically desirable in social life for the sake of human relations, but also spiritually indispensable with regard to self-cultivation and self-preservation. As for the doctrine of retreat as contrasted with advance, it does not encourage people to withdraw from society, as is often misconceived. Instead, it advises people not to flaunt intelligence and successes, as this will surely bring about disaster. These themes are notably presented in chapters 8, 9, 24 and 45 (DDJ).

15. On Knowledge and Wisdom

Lao Zi makes a distinction between general knowledge and true wisdom. He holds a negative stance on the former, as he thinks it could be possibly superficial and even pretentious. But he gives much credit to the latter since he believes that it is closely associated with the *Dao* as the origin of all things. It is observable that the approach to wisdom proposed by Lao Zi features honesty, modesty, purity, sincerity, self-knowledge, and simplicity. To be scrutinized with regard to this theme are chapters 33, 47, 52, 56 and 71 (DDJ).

16. On Fortune and Misfortune

Good fortune or happiness is what all people hanker after. At the same time, misfortune or misery is what people try to avoid. However, they go hand in hand as though in a kind of twinship. Being two opposites in unity, they are mutually interdependent and transformational. This emerges in Lao Zi's dialectical thinking as expressed in Chapter 58 (DDJ).

17. On Life and Death

The conceptions of life and death are crucially important to all human beings. Almost all philosophers, east or west, were and are preoccupied one way or another with various and respective perspectives on life and death. Lao Zi, as the founder of *Dao*ism, asserts that both life and death are as natural as anything else in the world. Zhuang Zi, who inherits this attitude, thinks that they are neither to be welcomed nor rejected. Therefore, these two thinkers advise people to view life and death as nothing but natural phenomena to the extent that the former is not to be overvalued and the latter not to be feared. The best way to preserve life is, according to Lao Zi, to live out one's natural term free from cares and worries. This could be possible only when one sees through the value of life and the nature of death. Please look at Chapter 50 (DDJ) and some relevant ideas of Zhuang Zi.

18. On the Merits of Contentment

A saying widespread among the Chinese people goes: "He who is contented (with what he has) is always merry and happy." This notion is in fact derived from Lao Zi's view on the causes of social problems in his own day. His recommendation of contentment, or self-contentment, if properly interpreted and received, still has a certain instructive import in modern times, when society is just as obsessed with material desires as in Lao Zi's time. The focus of the discussion falls on chapters 44 and 46 (DDJ).

19. On the Possibilities of Achievement

Lao Zi is often misunderstood as an advocator of 'doing nothing' or "non-action", through which one is expected to abstain from society or reject any social role. The fact of the matter is that Lao Zi keeps advising people to take no (arbitrary) action, follow the *Dao* of spontaneity or being-thus (ziran), and act for others but not compete with them. A close reading of chapters 63 and 64 (DDJ) will help one grasp Lao Zi's notion of so-called "doing nothing" (wu wei) at all.

20. On the Art of Leadership

Lao Zi's political philosophy is amply reflected in

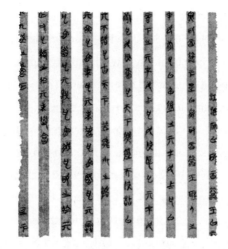

his discussion of the art of leadership. Generally speaking, it features "take-no-action," "non-competition," "retreat for the sake of advance," and "keeping to tenderness as a strategy." Driven or stimulated by their experiences and practical demands, many readers of the *Dao De Jing* project their own ideas or read modern themes into the book. That is why it is continually read and reread and new discoveries are constantly surfacing. Scrutiny of the following 11 chapters (DDJ) will illustrate this.

21. On Warfare

The *Dao De Jing* is taken by some people (e.g. Mao Zedong) to be a book filled with military thoughts and strategies, in spite of the fact that Lao Zi himself generally maintains a negative attitude to warfare. In the military arena, Lao Zi proposes a defensive policy that is firmly based on his notion of retreat as advance. Developed from this defensive policy are such military strategies and tactics as "wait at one's ease for an exhausted enemy," "defend in order to attack," and "retreat in order to advance," which are all intended to "gain mastery or win victory by striking only after the enemy has struck." In addition, Lao Zi's exposure of the interactions between the "normal way" (*zheng*) and the "unusual or extraordinary way" (*qi*) contains a rich dialectical message and character. Chapters 57, 68 and 69 (DDJ) also touch upon this theme.

22. On Peace

Lao Zi values peace and stability more than anything else in the social domain. This is reflected in his staunch anti-war attitude. Thus he regards weapons as instruments of evil that may be used only when there is no other alternative. He emphasizes that the use of military force is dangerous, for "as soon as great wars are over, years of famine are sure to afflict the land." Accordingly he denounces all excessive military operations and discourages any delight in military victory. In addition, he even goes so far as to advise the winning side to cherish humanism by mourning the multitudes killed in the fighting. Lao Zi's argument on pre-war and post-war peace is presented in chapters 30 and 31 (DDJ).

23. On Returning to Antiquity

Lao Zi assumes that primeval society was characterized by peace, harmony and stability because the ancients acted in accordance with the *Dao* and embraced simplicity and integrity. Appalled at the social problems and chaotic political situation of his own time, Lao Zi hankers for the "good old days" of antiquity, where, he implies, solutions to contemporary problems can be found. The relevant chapters are 17, 18, 19 and 65 (DDJ).

24. On the Ideal Society

Throughout his book, Lao Zi proposes the principle of the *Dao*, advocates simplicity of mind, appreciates the environment of tranquility, denounces the catastrophe of war and admires antiquity. All these elements naturally lead to his conception of the ideal society, featuring "a small state with few people." It is ostensibly out of the range of feasibility or possibility. It is therefore taken as a spiritual refuge for those who tend to frown upon over-civilization and shun the problematic world. All this is chiefly exposed in Chapter 80.

25. The Attitude to the *Dao-De*

There are generally three different kinds of attitudes toward the *Dao-De* categorized by Lao Zi. The first is positive and held by the highest type of *shi* (literati); the second is doubtful and held by the average type of *shi*; the last is negative and held by the lowest type of *shi*. Personal cultivation in *Dao*ism depends, first and foremost, on an appropriate attitude to the *Dao-De*. Close reading of chapters 41 and 70 (DDJ) may give one some basic ideas about this.

26. The Experience of the *Dao-De*

As a result of adopting a positive attitude to the *Dao-De*, one would undergo a highly enlightened experience and change of mentality that is uniquely distinct from and well transcends any practical or empirical types. This kind of experience and mentality feature above all simplicity, tranquility, genuineness, modesty, adaptability, open-mindedness and persistency, etc., which in turn represent the fundamental aspects of the ideal personality Lao Zi promotes. A scrutiny of chapters 15 and 20 (DDJ) will offer some insights into this subject.

27. The Praxis of the *Dao-De*

The praxis of the *Dao* and *De* involves relevant strategies articulated in the following chapter. The benefits of acting upon the *Dao* as the supreme principle and nourishing as the highest virtue are extensive and boundless according to Lao Zi; better still, they are accessible and available to all beings alike under Heaven. Remember to focus on chapters 7, 23 and 27, with reference to chapters 35, 52 and 54 (DDJ).

28. The Attainment of the *Dao-De*

It is notable that Lao Zi talks about the *Dao* from various perspectives throughout his book. Relatively speaking, one of the most important objectives lies in how to pursue the *Dao* as the highest sphere or realm of the human spirit. As a matter of fact, the pursuit of the *Dao* is implied in certain hidden proposals as suggested in his discussion of the *Dao* and its characteristics. It is worth mentioning that the pursuit of the *Dao* reflects the Daoist ideal of human life. In order to illustrate Lao Zi's concept of attaining the *Dao*, we presume to break down his proposed approach to the *Dao-De* into six dimensional components as follows:

(1) self-purification and deep contemplation;

(2) plainness and simplicity;

(3) vacuity and tranquility;

(4) tenderness and non-competition;

(5) have-less-selfishness and have-few-desires;

(6) naturalness and take-no-action.

The focus of the discussion can be found in chapters 10, 13, 16, 22, 28 and 49 (DDJ).

(1) Self-purification and Deep Contemplation

This subtitle is a modified version of Lao Zi's notion (i.e. di chu xuan jian) initially presented in Chapter 10 (DDJ). One may as well go on to read chapters 47 and 52 (DDJ) so as to achieve a better understanding of how to purify one's mind and contemplate things in a similar form of insightful meditation or observation. The approach as such is, needless to say, oriented toward the mastery of and the nourishment of the *De*.

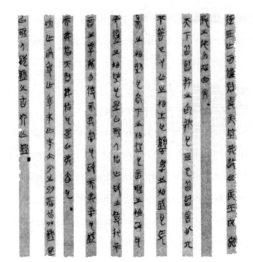

(2) Plainness and Simplicity

This subtitle stresses the perception of plainness and the embracing of simplicity (*jian su bao pu*). It is taken directly from Chapter 19 of the *Dao De Jing* and is proposed by Lao Zi himself as an approach to the attainment of the *Dao*. As a matter of fact, simplicity is another name for the *Dao*, which features naturalness, innocence and purity. It seems minute, simple and clumsy, yet, it can be so powerful that nothing under Heaven can subdue it. Therefore, if the rulers were able to maintain it, all the people would submit to them spontaneously. Examine what Lao Zi says about this in Chapter 28 (DDJ).

(3) Vacuity and Tranquility

Vacuity and tranquility (*xuji shoujing*) are recommended by Lao Zi as two major principles for self-cultivation on the one hand, and for the attainment of the *Dao* and the nourishment of the *De* on the other. The application of these two principles is expected to purify the mind of all conventional prejudices and egoistic desires. At the same time, one can free oneself from all self-indulgence and external disturbances as well as material temptations. By so doing one is able to return to the root as the state of tranquility, to the destiny as the originally good nature, and to the eternal as the everlasting and supreme principle of the *Dao*. As a consequence, he will be one, or identified with the *Dao* and Heaven; that is, he will then achieve the highest form of life in a spiritual sense. Perceive Lao Zi's argument presented in Chapter 16 (DDJ).

(4) Tenderness and Non-competition

Lao Zi firmly grounds his doctrine of keeping to tenderness (*shourou*) on his conviction that "Reversion is the movement of the *Dao*." Thus he believes that the tender, soft and weak are companions of life and able to overcome the hard, stiff and strong, described as companions of death in his terminology. Conquest of this kind is only possible in Lao Zi's opinion when the *De* of non-competition (*buzheng*) is concretely applied as a code of conduct to practice with sincerity and modesty. It requires therefore such indispensable traits as "not clinging to one's opinions," "not claiming to be always right" and "not boasting of one's prowess," which are all stressed in Chapter 22 (DDJ).

(5) Have-less-selfishness and Have-few-desires

Presented in Chapter 19 (DDJ) is the idea of reducing one's selfishness and having few desires (*shaosi guayu*) in order to approach the *Dao* as the model for the world. As has been read in his book, Lao Zi respectively recommends having less selfishness by forgetting one's body and having few desires by developing a state of infancy. If one's self-cultivation reaches this stage, one is well on the path to the attainment of the *Dao* and *De* together. First examine Chapter 13 (DDJ), and then chapter 49 (DDJ).

(6) Naturalness and Take-no-action

Lao Zi proclaims that the *Dao* follows naturalness or spontaneity (*ziran*, cf. chs. 25 and 22, DDJ) and features take-no-action (*wuwei*, cf. chs. 37, 38 and 48, DDJ). In turn, we may as well take them as an approach to achieving the *Dao*. The application of this approach can be effective only when the pursuit of the *Dao* is firmly established as the ultimate goal of life. A relevant and instructive message is contained in Chapter 48 (DDJ).

图书在版编目（CIP）数据

道德经／（春秋）老子著；王柯平译.
－北京：外文出版社，2003.9
ISBN 978-7-119-03445-4

I.道... II.①老... ②王... III.道家－英文Ⅳ.B223.11

中国版本图书馆 CIP 数据核字（2003）第 085228 号

责任编辑　　贾先锋
封面设计　　华子图文
内文设计　　一瓢设计·邱特聪
印刷监制　　冯　浩

道 德 经

（春秋）老子　著

王柯平　译

*

© 外文出版社

外文出版社出版

（中国北京百万庄大街 24 号）

邮政编码　100037

外文出版社网址：http://www.flp.com.cn

北京外文印刷厂印刷

中国国际图书贸易总公司发行

（中国北京车公庄西路 35 号）

北京邮政信箱第 399 号　邮政编码　100044

2008 年(32 开)第 1 版

2008 年第 1 版第 1 次印刷

（英）

ISBN 978-7-119-03445-4

04800

7-E-3586 P